Dec 2014

Dwyane Wade

SUPERSTARS IN THE WORLD OF BASKETBALL

SUPERSTARS IN THE WORLD OF BASKETBALL

Dwyane Wade

Aurelia Jackson

Mason Crest

Mason Crest
450 Parkway Drive, Suite D
Broomall, PA 19008
www.masoncrest.com

Printed and bound in the United States of America.

First printing
9 8 7 6 5 4 3 2 1

Series ISBN: 978-1-4222-3101-2
ISBN: 978-1-4222-3106-7
ebook ISBN: 978-1-4222-8796-5

The Library of Congress has cataloged the
hardcopy format(s) as follows:
        Library of Congress Cataloging-in-Publication Data

Jackson, Aurelia.
   Dwyane Wade / Aurelia Jackson.
      pages cm. — (Superstars in the world of basketball)
   ISBN 978-1-4222-3106-7 (hardback) — ISBN 978-1-4222-3101-2 (series) — ISBN 978-1-4222-8796-5 (ebook) 1. Wade, Dwyane, 1982—Juvenile literature. 2. Basketball players—United States—Biography—Juvenile literature. I. Title.
   GV884.W23J33 2015
   796.323092—dc23
   [B]
                                        2014007848

Contents

KEY ICONS TO LOOK FOR:

 Text-Dependent Questions: These questions send the reader back to the text for more careful attention to the evidence presented there.

 Words to Understand: These words with their easy-to-understand definitions will increase the reader's understanding of the text, while building vocabulary skills.

 Series Glossary of Key Terms: This back-of-the book glossary contains terminology used throughout this series. Words found here increase the reader's ability to read and comprehend higher-level books and articles in this field.

 Research Projects: Readers are pointed toward areas of further inquiry connected to each chapter. Suggestions are provided for projects that encourage deeper research and analysis.

 Sidebars: This boxed material within the main text allows readers to build knowledge, gain insights, explore possibilities, and broaden their perspectives by weaving together additional information to provide realistic and holistic perspectives.

Words to Understand

qualify: Do well enough to compete in a final round or contest.
dedicated: Devoted.
mission: Goal.
aspirations: Hopes to one day achieve something great.
militant: Very aggressive and strict.

Starting at the Bottom

Dwyane Wade sprints across the basketball court floor. The Miami Heat is facing the San Antonio Spurs in the seventh and final game of the 2013 NBA Finals. Time is almost up and the scores are very close. It's still anybody's game! Dwyane and his teammates are tired and covered in sweat, but they can't rest just yet. They need to keep working their hardest to snag victory.

The Miami Heat and the San Antonio Spurs have worked hard to reach this point. The best teams in the NBA need to *qualify* for the playoffs before they are allowed to play in the finals. After winning enough games, the two best teams face each other in a series of final games. In 2012, the Miami Heat won their first championship since 2006. Now, one year later, Dwyane and his teammates hope to win again—but there's just one problem. The San Antonio Spurs are just as talented, and they don't plan to let the Heat win easily!

With the clock counting down, the Heat manages to score a few more times. The final score is 95 to 88 when the bell sounds. The Miami Heat has won by just seven points! The crowd goes wild as teammates cheer and hug each other. Fans of the Heat who are

Dwyane Wade is one of the best players on the Miami Heat, but he can't take credit for everything they've accomplished. It's because of the Heat's strong teamwork that they've been so successful in recent years.

DWYANE WADE

sitting in the stands jump to their feet and shout in celebration. Confetti falls from the ceiling, covering everyone in the stadium. Opponents shake hands and congratulate each other on a good game.

The members of the Miami Heat have a lot to make them proud. Not only have they won the NBA championship, but they have done it two years in a row. These victories do not belong to just one player alone. Basketball is a team sport. The best basketball players in the world know that they need to work with their teammates in order to win. They cannot be selfish with the ball. Dwyane and his teammates pass around the ball a lot on the court. It doesn't matter who shoots for the basket as long as the team earns points. In the last game alone, Dwyane scored 23 points for his team. He also helped others earn points as well.

Becoming an NBA champion is a great accomplishment, but this year was extra special for Dwyane. It was his third NBA championship victory, which put him in a special category with some of the best basketball players in history.

A few days after the NBA finals, Dwyane was asked how he felt about the victory. He said, "It's kind of hard to put in words, you know, to think about where I come from, to think about where my family comes from. And to be here, not only in the NBA, but to celebrate my third championship."

Dwyane overcame a lot of challenges as he was growing up. Dealing with poverty was one of them. With some help from his family, though, Dwyane was able to get a better education and move up in the world. He worked hard and stayed *dedicated* to the sport of basketball. Eventually, he went to college and fulfilled his dream of playing basketball in the NBA. He has also played on the United States Olympic basketball team twice, winning a bronze medal in 2004 and a gold medal in 2008.

EARLY LIFE WITH MOM

Dwyane Tyrone Wade Jr. was born on January 17, 1982. He grew up in Chicago, Illinois. When Dwyane was very young, his parents separated and later divorced. For the first few

Chicago, where Dwyane grew up, has some very poor and dangerous neighborhoods. If he was going to live up to his full potential, Tragil knew she needed to get Dwyane to a better life.

years of his life, Dwyane lived with his mother, Jolinda. His older sister Tragil also lived with them. She is five years older than Dwyane. Dwyane and Tragil didn't get to see their father very often while they were living with Jolinda.

Life for Jolinda, Dwyane, and Tragil was not easy. Jolinda did not have anyone to help her support her family. She had to do it all by herself. It was hard for her to find a place to live that she could afford. The family moved around a lot. They lived in some of the poorest neighborhoods in Chicago.

When Dwyane still lived with his mother, he was exposed to many dangers. There were gangs and drug dealers on the streets where he lived. People who are in gangs sometimes commit violent crimes. The neighborhoods Dwyane lived in were so unsafe that he could sometimes hear gunshots at night as a child. The dangers of the streets were not Dwyane's only problem, though. His own mother used illegal drugs. If Dwyane had not eventually left his mother's care, he might have ended up following in her footsteps.

Dwyane had a lot of goals growing up. "It was my *mission* as a young kid to overcome being poor. I had so many dreams, so many *aspirations*," Dwyane has said. Wanting to be successful and actually doing it are two different things, however. In order to become the famous basketball player he is today, Dwyane needed to keep working at it. His dedication to basketball began when he was a child and has been going strong ever since.

MOVING IN WITH DAD

When Dwyane was nine years old, Tragil knew she needed to get Dwyane out of his mother's care. The only way to do this would be to bring Dwyane to his father's house.

Getting Dwyane to leave his mother would not be easy, though. Tragil would have to trick him into it. One day, she did just that. Tragil took Dwyane on a bus and told him that they would be going to the movies. Instead, she took him to the neighborhood where their father was living. Tragil dropped Dwyane off at their father's house and went back home. From that point forward, Dwyane lived with his father.

Tragil chose to bring Dwyane to his father's house because she wanted to give him a better life. She knew that Dwyane living with their mother would only hurt him in the long run. If Dwyane didn't leave his mother's care, he might get dragged into using or dealing drugs. Before moving in with his father, Dwyane had no father figure or male role models in his life. Tragil thought he needed some older family members to look up to. His older stepbrothers would be a good influence.

At first, Dwyane didn't know that Tragil would not come back for him. "It was two days before I realized she wasn't coming back," he said. "She was trying to get me away from the gangs and drugs, which was outside in our faces every day, right in front of our mother's house. She didn't want me to get caught up in it." Tragil was only thirteen years old when she decided that Dwyane would be better off in their father's care.

When Dwyane was young, Michael Jordan was one of the most famous basketball players in the world. Many of today's basketball stars started out because they were inspired by the amazing things Michael Jordan was able to do on the court.

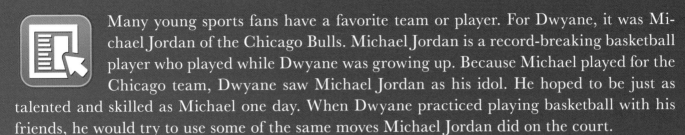
By the time Dwyane moved in with his father, his father had remarried another woman. Dwyane now had a stepmother and a few new stepsiblings. Dwyane's father was very strict compared to Jolinda. He gave Dwyane Jr. and the rest of his children the direction they needed in life. "My father was **militant**. He kept us out of a lot of trouble because we respected his 'no's' and 'don'ts'," Dwyane said. Discipline wasn't the only thing Dwyane's father gave him, though. Dwyane Sr. also encouraged his children to play sports. If it weren't for his father's influence, Dwyane might not have discovered his love for basketball.

A year after Dwyane arrived at his father's house, the whole family moved to Robbins, Illinois. Robbins is a town on the south side of Chicago. It wasn't the best neighborhood, but it was a huge step up from where Dwyane had been living with his mother. Moving to Robbins gave the family more room to play outside. The young Dwyane liked to play

Even when he was young, basketball was a central part of Dwyane's life. He played with his stepbrothers, and his father was a basketball coach.

Text-Dependent Questions

1. How many points did Dwyane score in the last game of the 2013 NBA Finals?
2. Why were the neighborhoods that Dwyane lived in as a child so unsafe?
3. Why did Tragil feel that Dwyane should live with his father instead of his mother?
4. How old was Tragil when she brought Dwyane to live with his father?
5. How did Dwyane's father keep him out of trouble?

basketball with his stepbrothers and father. His father even coached a basketball team at the local recreational center.

Living with his father changed Dwyane's life forever. "Moving in with my dad at the age of nine was probably the most important part of my life," Dwyane told the *Huffington Post*. "That was at the point and the age that I needed a male voice. I needed the discipline. I needed someone to look at and say, 'I want to be like you.'" Now that Dwyane was living with his father and stepbrothers, he had some male role models to look up to. This sort of guidance gave Dwyane the strength he needed to do well in sports and especially basketball.

Words to Understand

excelling: Doing very well at.

selective: Picky about who is chosen.

competitive: Having to do with a situation like a school or job where people must prove how good they are in order to be let in.

recruiting: Choosing someone to play on a team.

media: Ways of getting information to lots of people at once, like the news or the Internet.

STAYING IN SCHOOL

As a young boy, Dwyane dreamed of one day playing as a professional basketball player. Like any other hopeful athlete, he quickly learned that you can't become a pro overnight. He needed to keep practicing to become an expert. Dwyane began training hard in elementary school and continued to work on his skills until he entered high school. He attended Harold L. Richards High School in Oak Lawn, a suburb of Chicago.

HIGH SCHOOL

After Dwyane entered high school, he tried out for the varsity basketball team. Varsity teams are very picky. An athlete who wants to join the team must try out before he or she can join. The best players from the tryouts are then put on the varsity team. Dwyane made the cut and began playing in his second year of high school.

Even though Dwyane was a good player for his age, his coach didn't give him a lot

Basketball was the sport that Dwayne was best at, and that he would go on to make a career out of—but he was also good at football and played both games in high school.

of time on the court. Dwyane was still young and inexperienced compared to the other players. His older stepbrother Demetris, on the other hand, was the star of the basketball team. Dwyane would just have to wait for his turn to shine. Until then, he would focus on becoming a better player.

Many athletes are good at several different sports. Dwyane was no exception. Basketball would always be Dwyane's first love, but he enjoyed playing football, too. In high school, he was the wide receiver of the football team. At the same time, Dwyane continued to practice his basketball skills. By the time he reached his junior year, he was a lot taller and much better at handling the ball on the court. He had grown four inches over the summer and was now over six feet tall. At this height, he was ready to challenge any high school student on the court.

In Dwyane's junior year, his basketball coach gave him the chance to prove himself. Dwyane worked very hard to earn more playing time and it showed. That year, Dwyane averaged about 20 points per game on his own. In Dwyane's senior year, his point average increased to 27 points per game. It was clear at this point that Dwyane was no longer living in his stepbrother's shadow. Instead, Dwyane had taken Demetris' place as the star of the team.

The Harold L. Richards High School basketball team did very well that year. With Dwyane's help, the team ended the season with twenty-four victories and only five losses. By the end of the season, Dwyane had also broken a school record. He had become the only person from his school to ever score 676 points and 106 steals throughout just one season.

Although Dwyane was *excelling* at basketball, he was having a lot of problems in his personal life. At home, his father and stepmother were fighting a lot. These arguments were distracting for Dwyane. His grades suffered because it was so hard to concentrate on school work while he was at home. Dwyane did well in class, but his test scores were not good. Some of his teachers noticed this and tried to help him out by tutoring him.

Dwyane chose Marquette University partly because of how close it was to home. Even though he couldn't play for their basketball team at first, he practiced with the team and stayed in shape, so he would be ready to play as soon as his grades were up.

All official sports, including basketball, have rules that players must follow. Most of these rules have to do with how the game is played. Some special rules control what athletes can and can't do when they are off the court. At the professional level, these rules are made by the NBA. For college athletes, the rules are created by the National Collegiate Athlete Association (NCAA). One of these many rules states that all athletes who compete at the college level must have completed a certain amount of high school credits. Completing enough courses is not enough, however. A student needs to get good grades on tests, too. This special rule is known as Proposition 48. Dwyane could not play basketball during his first year of college because he did not meet the requirements of Proposition 48.

In Dwyane's senior year, his high school girlfriend, Siohvaughn, went away to go to college. While she was gone, he visited Siohvaughn's mother Darlene. When Darlene found out what Dwyane was going through at home and in school, she offered to let him stay at her house. Darlene's help made Dwyane's senior year just a little easier to handle.

GOING TO COLLEGE

Some basketball players choose to go straight from high school to the NBA, but not Dwyane. He wanted to get an education and play his favorite sport at the same time. Like Dwyane's high school, many colleges have a *selective* basketball team. Some college basketball teams are so good that they get to play all over the country. This can be exciting for someone like Dwyane who hadn't opportunities to travel a lot.

College basketball is very *competitive*, but Dwyane had no problem being noticed as a great addition to any team. Unfortunately, his poor grades in high school almost held him back. Not many colleges wanted to risk *recruiting* Dwyane because of his poor grades. Only Marquette University, Illinois State University, and DePaul University invited Dwyane to join their basketball teams.

Dwyane decided to go to Marquette University in Milwaukee, Wisconsin. It takes about an hour to drive from Chicago to Marquette. Because it is so close to where Dwyane grew up, he would be able to visit home as often as he liked. Dwyane chose to study broadcasting in college.

Being in college was not easy for Dwyane. In his first year at Marquette University, he was unable to play basketball because of how poorly he did in his high school classes. Even though Dwyane could not play for the Marquette Golden Eagles, his coach did let

Tim Creane, above, was always hard on Dwyane, but it was because he believed in Dwyane and always knew he could do better. Without Tom's tough love, Dwyane might not have achieved everything that he has today!

him practice with the team. Coach Tom Crean did this to help Dwyane prepare for future games. He knew Dwyane was something special, and he didn't want to give up on him. Dwyane proved Coach Crean right by getting the help he needed.

Before Dwyane was allowed to officially play basketball on the college team, he would need to complete a few college courses. The first step was finding a tutor. Over time, Dwyane was able to improve his writing. Thanks to his tutoring sessions, he learned how to easily explain his ideas on paper. Dwyane started to do well on tests and finally qualified to join the college basketball team.

Dwyane wasted no time showing what he was made of in his second year of college. He averaged about 18 points per game. The Golden Eagles finished the season with twenty-six wins and seven losses at the end of the 2001–2002 season. This was the best record the school had achieved since 1994.

Dwyane plays as a guard, which means that he needs to be fast on his feet and able to pass quickly to his teammates.

Text-Dependent Questions

1. Why didn't Dwyane get a lot of time on the court when he first joined his high school's varsity basketball team?
2. Was basketball the only sport Dwyane played in high school?
3. Why did Dwyane start doing poorly in school in his junior year?
4. Why didn't Dwyane go straight to the NBA when he graduated from high school?
5. What is a triple-double?

In Dwyane's next year of college, he showed no signs of slowing down! His average points per game just kept getting better. By the end of the season, Dwyane had averaged over 21 points per game. That year, the Golden Eagles made it to the semi-finals of the national championship for the first time since 1977. In a game against the Kentucky Wildcats, Dwyane scored a triple-double. To do this, he scored 29 points, 11 rebounds, and 11 assists in a single game. A triple-double is when any basketball player scores double digits in any three categories of basketball statistics.

Dwyane's amazing performance that year did not go unnoticed. His hard work earned him a place on the All-American First Team. This team is made up of the most skilled basketball players at the college level. Sports fans and the *media* vote on who will be included. Although the team does not actually play together, it is still a great honor to be named an All-American Athlete.

When it came time to start his fourth year at Marquette University, Dwyane needed to make a choice. He had become very popular after he had done so well on the court the year before. Many sports fans even believed he was ready to join the NBA. His dream had always been to play basketball professionally, and now he had the chance. Dwyane thought long and hard about his decision before he chose to leave Marquette in order to enter the 2003 NBA draft. Players who sign up for a draft agree to join a professional team if they are picked.

Dwyane was chosen in the draft by the Miami Heat, a team based in Miami, Florida. Dwyane would need to be there to practice and play for most of the year. Unlike Marquette and Chicago, Chicago and Miami are very far apart. It would not be easy to be far away from home, but Dwyane knew this was something he had to do. To succeed in the world of basketball, he would need to make certain sacrifices.

Words to Understand

qualified: Met all necessary requirements.

MOVING UP

Before Dwyane even began playing for the Miami Heat, the team had high hopes for him. Of all the players entering the draft, Dwyane was chosen fifth overall. That year, he became one of only four Marquette players in history to ever be picked in the first round. Of those four players, Dwyane was chosen the fastest.

OFF TO A ROUGH START

When Dwyane first joined the Miami Heat, the team was not doing very well. Heat fans hoped that Dwyane would help put the team back on the map. In his first season as a professional basketball player, Dwyane was a rookie. Rookies are new to the NBA. They usually don't do as well as more experienced players. In his rookie year, Dwyane averaged about 16 points, 4 rebounds, and 4 assists per game. His performance was enough to put him in the running for the Rookie of the Year award. He placed third behind LeBron James and Carmelo Anthony.

Shaquille O'Neal played for the NBA for nineteen years. During this time, he became one of the most experienced players on the court—and Dwyane learned a lot from playing with him.

Even with Dwyane on the team, the Heat had a rough start. It can take some time for a basketball player to get used to playing with new teammates. By the end of the season, the team improved a lot. The Heat finished with forty-two wins and forty losses. This meant that the team won about half of the games played. These victories **qualified** the Heat for the NBA playoffs. Unfortunately, the Heat did not win the championship that year, but the experience of making it to the playoffs gave Dwyane and his teammates the drive to do even better next year.

GETTING BETTER

Basketball players would be nothing without their teammates. Working together is a very important part of scoring. One teammate can pass the ball to another in order to make a clear shot at the basket. Talented basketball players can help each other improve and help a team do better in the NBA. In 2004, Dwyane was given the chance to play with someone very famous. Shaquille O'Neal joined the Miami Heat team. Shaquille is much older than Dwyane and very skilled.

Playing with Shaq would be a great honor and learning experience for Dwyane, but it wasn't one-sided. Shaquille had noticed how well Dwyane was doing on the Miami Heat and wanted a chance to play alongside him. That year, the Miami Heat won forty-two games and made it to the playoffs. Dwyane was also selected to be a reserve player in the 2005 NBA All-Star Game. Reserves are called in when the main players are tired. Even though he only played for twenty-four minutes, Dwyane scored 14 points for his team.

Dwyane's third year playing for the Heat went even better than the first two. He was selected for his second All-Star Game and helped lead his team to a 122–120 victory. The Miami Heat made it to the NBA finals and won with the help of Dwyane. This was the first

The 2006 finals were hard for the Miami Heat—at one point they were trailing two games behind the Dallas Mavericks. In the end, though, they came back and won after six games, with Dwyane being named MVP.

of three championships Dwyane would win. By the end of the season, it was clear that all of Dwyane's hard work had paid off. He was named the Most Valuable Player (MVP) of the NBA Finals in 2006.

INJURY AND ILLNESS

Playing sports puts a lot of stress on an athlete's body. Practicing every day and playing often will wear down anyone. Athletes can get sick just like the rest of us. Professionals like Dwyane will keep pushing themselves, even when they are ill. If Dwyane does not play, he is letting more than himself down. He would be letting down his teammates and his fans, too.

Dedication is an important quality in any basketball player. Dwyane proved time and time again that he was willing to go above and beyond what was required of him. He has played in NBA games while dealing with many different illnesses and injuries. Some of the illnesses include a sinus infection and the flu. Playing basketball is already difficult enough. Playing with a runny nose, a terrible cough, and a fever is even harder! Fortunately, most sickness is curable with medicine. With enough rest, someone who is sick will get better in a week or two. Injuries take much longer to heal.

Playing sports comes with many risks. Basketball players are injured on the court all the time. A common cause of injury is falling down or bumping into another player. Dwyane is no stranger to being injured while playing. Throughout his career, he has injured many body parts, including his knee, his calf, his hip, and his shoulder.

Dwyane tries not to let these injuries slow him down. If a game is really important, Dwyane will keep playing until it is over before seeking medical attention. Sometimes, he is forced to stop. Once he needed to be taken off of the court in a wheelchair following an injury. Dwyane had dislocated his shoulder while trying to steal the ball from an opponent.

Unlike illnesses, injuries can take months to heal. More serious injuries might even require surgery. When Dwyane injured his shoulder in 2007, he knew it would not ever

Dwyane didn't want to take time off from the game he loved, even though he was injured. In 2007, he realized that his injury was getting worse and it was time to take some time off to deal with it.

It is no secret that most basketball players are very tall. The extra height helps players shoot for a basket and block opponents from scoring. Some basketball players can even jump to dunk the basketball straight into the hoop! As far as basketball players go, Dwyane is an average size. He is just six feet and four inches tall. Blocking an opponent from scoring can be hard if the opponent's arms can reach higher. When Dwyane blocked one hundred shots in the 2008–2009 season, he became the first person shorter than 6'5" to block one hundred shots in a season.

completely heal without surgery. With the season in progress, he chose to put off the surgery until later. Even without surgery, Dwyane still needed time to rest and heal his injury. He missed over thirty games that season because of it.

Later that year, Dwyane realized he could not put off fixing his body any longer. He underwent surgery for his shoulder and knee injuries. He planned to have the surgeries during the off season so that he would not miss too many games.

Resting after surgery is important. The injured area needs time to heal. Dwyane was not able to move his shoulder or his knee for months after surgery. Unfortunately, resting can have negative consequences too. A body part can become weak if it isn't exercised regularly. The muscles in Dwyane's shoulder and knee needed to be strengthened before he could play basketball again. This is known as rehabilitation.

Even with physical therapy and months of rest, Dwyane's injures continued to give him problems. An injury that keeps coming back is known as a chronic injury. Dwyane missed even more games to undergo a different kind of treatment for his knee injury. At the end of that year, Dwyane had averaged over 24 points per game. That's not bad for someone with a chronic injury!

Research Project

In 2005, Dwyane was chosen as a reserve player in the NBA All-Star Game. Go online and find some more information about the All-Star Game. What is the All-Star Game? How is it different from a normal NBA game between two teams? Who are some of the other players who have been chosen to play? Was Dwyane chosen for any All-Star Games since 2005?

In the NBA All-Star Game, the best players from the Eastern Conference go head-to-head with the best players from the Western Conference. Here, Dwyane and his Eastern-Conference teammates get ready to play.

A RECORD BREAKER

From 2008 to 2010, Dwyane kept improving his game. He had not done well because of his injuries, but now was his chance to make a comeback. Dwyane set a new record when he became the first player in NBA history to score 2,000 points, 500 assists, and 150 steals in a single season. That year, Dwyane also played in his fifth All-Star Game. The Miami Heat made it to the NBA playoffs again but did not win.

Text-Dependent Questions

1. What is a rookie? Why don't they usually do as well as other players?
2. Who is Shaquille O'Neal? How did having him play on the Miami Heat help Dwyane become a better player?
3. Why are injuries and illnesses especially bad for a professional athlete?
4. Why did Dwyane miss so many games, even after he had surgery to fix his injuries?
5. What were Dwyane's averages during the 2009-2010 basketball season?

At this point, Dwyane was known as one of the best players in the league. He continued to break more records. By the end of the season, Dwyane scored an average of 30 points per game. He was awarded the NBA Scoring Title because of it. In the 2009–2010 season, Dwyane celebrated a milestone in his career. Since joining the NBA, he had scored a total of 10,000 points. Not many NBA players have ever reached this point.

Overall, Dwyane's statistics dropped slightly in this season. He scored an average of about 26 points and 7 assists per game. Although his statistics for 2009-2010 were not as good as the year before, that did not keep Dwyane from having some great games. In the playoffs, Dwyane broke a personal record when he scored an impressive 46 points against the Boston Celtics in the playoffs. This was the highest number of points he had ever scored in a single playoff game.

That year, the Heat came home empty-handed once again, though. Dwyane and his teammates had not won the championship, and some fans wondered if they ever would. All of that would change in the next year when two more rising stars were brought onto the Miami Heat team.

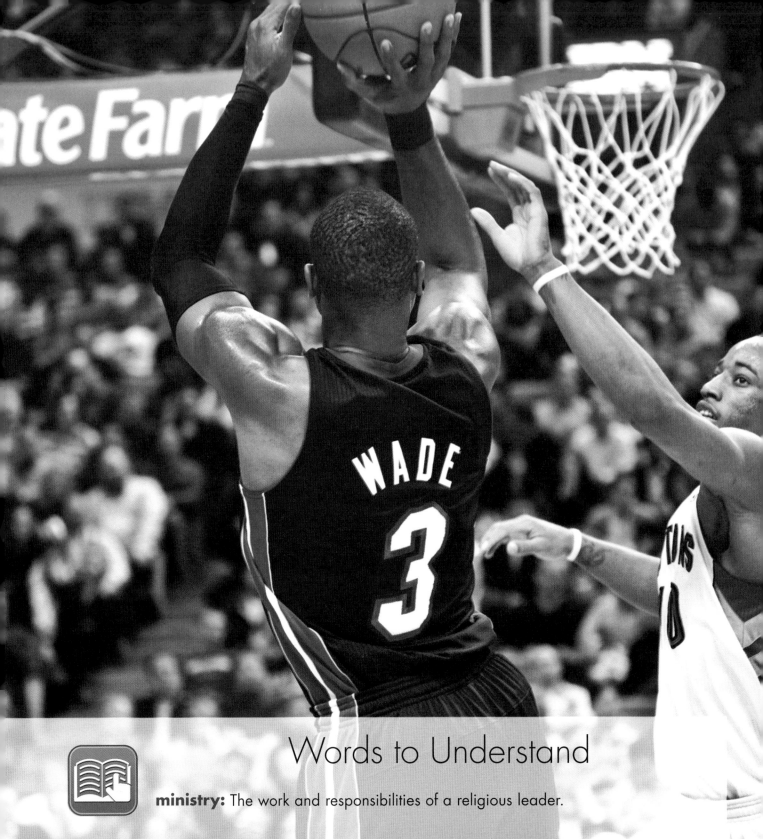

Words to Understand

LOOKING FORWARD

In 2010, Dwyane became a free agent. Free agents are not signed to any team. This gave Dwyane a choice. He could either stay with the Miami Heat or join another team. Many of Dwyane's loyal fans wanted him to stay with the Heat, but Dwyane had other reasons for wanting to stay. He had grown used to living in Miami and working with his teammates, but what really convinced Dwyane to stay was the promise of two new members.

THE BIG THREE

While Dwyane was playing for the Miami Heat all these years, LeBron James and Chris Bosh had been playing for different teams. LeBron was from the Cleveland Cavaliers while Chris was from the Toronto Raptors. Like Dwyane, these two players were very successful on their own teams. If Dwyane, LeBron, and Chris played on the same team, that team would be even better! All three players decided to sign with the Miami Heat in 2010 so

In December of 2012, Dwyane was suspended for one game because he had kicked another player in the groin. A player who is suspended is not allowed to play in any games for a certain amount of time. Dwyane claimed it was an accident on his Twitter account by saying, "I'm far from being a dirty player, and my intent was never to kick Ramon Sessions. I just reacted to the contact that I got from him."

LeBron James is another of the best players in the NBA. The combination of him, Dwyane Wade, and Chris Bosh on one team proved to be almost unstoppable.

that they could play together. From that point on, Dwyane, LeBron, and Chris were known as the Big Three.

Playing together on the Miami Heat was not the first time Dwyane, LeBron, and Chris had been teammates. All three had competed in the 2008 Olympic Games. They became Olympic gold medalists together. By 2010, the Big Three were ready to become NBA champions. The Heat won a total of fifty-eight games that season. Dwyane and his teammates also managed to make it to the NBA finals for the first time since winning in 2006. Unfortunately, they lost against the Dallas Mavericks. This defeat only made Dwyane want a victory even more. By next year, he would find a way to snag it.

The 2012 All-Star Game was a great success for Dwyane. He scored the third triple-double in the history of the All-Star Games. Michael Jordan did it first in 1997, and LeBron did it a year before Dwyane in 2011. It had taken Dwyane a long time, but he had finally achieved the same level of success as his childhood idol, Michael Jordan.

When the NBA playoffs began, the Heat started out with a bang and made it to the finals with ease. The final score against the Oklahoma City Thunder was four to one, which meant that the Heat had won the 2012 NBA championship! This was the second time Dwyane became an NBA champion. The last time he had won the title was in 2006.

In the summer of 2012, Dwyane needed to have surgery on his knee once more. He was forced to miss the 2012 Olympic Games because of it. By the start of the NBA season, Dwyane was ready to return to the court.

At the end of the 2012–2013 season, the Miami Heat reached the finals once more. Dwyane and his teammates won again, making this the second year in a row. Their opponents, the Antonio Spurs, put up a real fight. In the end, the Miami Heat was victorious with the final score being four wins to three. This was Dwyane's third time winning a championship. As of 2013, Dwyane showed no signs of retiring.

Dwyane and Gabrielle Union got engaged at the end of 2013.

PERSONAL LIFE

When athletes compete, they must keep their head in the game. They can't think about anything besides what is happening on the court. Like all athletes, Dwyane knows this very well. Even as his basketball career kept improving, he was having a lot of problems of his own. Dwyane did his best not to let it affect his game. Many of Dwyane's fans did not know the struggles he was dealing with because of how well he played.

Dwyane is used to being on display as his fans watch from around the world. His personal life, however, is something he usually keeps quiet. But athletes have families and relationships just like everybody else.

Dwyane proposed to his long-time girlfriend Siohvaughn while he was still in college. A year later, she became pregnant. This was at a point when Dwyane's career was really starting to take off. He hoped to enter the NBA draft soon. It would be difficult to be a good basketball player and a good father at the same time.

Being an athlete is not just about playing games. It is a full-time job. Athletes who play basketball have very long and tiring schedules. They must practice every day to become the best in the world. Dwyane needed to find time for his wife, his child, and his practice schedule. It would be hard, but he was determined to make it work.

Things didn't work out the way he had hoped, though. Dwyane and Siohvaughn's baby was born in 2002, the same year they were married. They had another baby in 2007. But their marriage was in trouble. The same year his second child was born, Dwyane filed for a divorce. The divorce was finalized in 2010, and Dwyane was given custody of his two children, Zaire and Zion. Parents who are given custody take care of their children and raise them. Zaire and Zion live with Dwyane in Miami. Dwyane's ex-wife Siohvaughn lives in Chicago, but her two children are allowed to visit her every now and then.

After Dwyane and Siohvaughn were divorced, Dwyane began to date Gabrielle Union. She is an actress and a basketball fan. She sometimes goes to watch Dwyane and the Heat play. The two got engaged at the end of 2013. They told fans online with a picture of Gabrielle's new engagement ring.

After the Heat won the 2013 NBA Championship, they met with President Barack Obama and had their pictures taken with him. Obama, a basketball fan, spent the time talking and joking with the players.

FAITH

Dwyane is a Christian who believes in God, Jesus, and the Holy Spirit. This is called the Trinity, and it's the reason that he chose the number three for his jersey.

Another belief of Christianity is that everyone should donate at least 10 percent of the money they earn each year to God. This is called tithing. Dwyane follows this rule and gives 10 percent of his earnings to a church in Chicago.

He isn't the only person in his family who takes religion seriously. His mother and siblings do as well. When Dwyane moved in with his father, his older sister Tragil stayed home with their mother. Many years later, in 2001, Tragil convinced their mother to go to church. At the time, Jolinda was still using and selling drugs. Going to church with Tragil helped Jolinda make the decision to turn her life around. She stopped using drugs and served a prison sentence she had been avoiding. While she was in prison, Jolinda tried to help other people make some positive changes in their lives like she had. She became a minister, someone who teaches others about Christianity.

Jolinda finally left prison in 2003. After that, she worked to start her own church. In 2007, it became known as the Temple of Praise Binding and Loosing Ministry. Dwyane saw how dedicated his mother was to her church, and he wanted to help her out. He was also very happy that she had improved her life so much. With some of the money he had earned through his basketball career, Dwyane bought his mother a church building for her **ministry**. It opened in 2008. On the day of its opening, Jolinda said, "Today is one of the highest of the highest moments in my life."

GIVING BACK

Basketball players earn a lot of money. What they do with that money is entirely up to them. Dwyane is incredibly thankful for everything he has in life and wants to give back to the community. In 2003, he founded the Wade's World Foundation. This organization helps children get the education they need to be successful. Each year, hundreds of thousands of dollars are given to different communities by his charity.

Starting large foundations isn't the only way Wade helps those around him. He also likes giving to individuals and smaller organizations, too. In 2009, he donated money to keep the Robbins, Illinois, library from closing. This library is very important to him because he grew up in the area. When a woman in Florida lost her house to an accidental fire, Dwyane helped her rebuild it. He also gave her family clothes and furniture.

Text-Dependent Questions

1. What is a free agent? What did it mean for Dwyane's basketball career?
2. Who were the Big Three?
3. Why did Dwyane pick the number three for his jersey?
4. What is tithing? How does Dwyane do it?
5. What is the Wade's World Foundation?

Sometimes, making a person's dream come true isn't about money. When Dwyane was seven years old, he saw a television program about celebrities who visited young children. At that moment, he vowed that he would do the same thing if he ever became famous. Today, Dwyane often visits sick children in hospitals to help brighten their days. Dwyane is known to give small presents to fans during basketball games. One time, he gave his jersey to an eight-year-old boy who had lost his hands and feet to an infection.

Dwyane Wade has been a part of the NBA for over ten years. In that time, he has become an NBA champion three times and an Olympic gold medalist. As successful as he is, he still hasn't gotten used to his popularity. "To me, it's still crazy when I walk around and I see people wearing my jersey, people wearing my shoes," said Dwyane. Even after all this time, Dwyane has stayed humble. He proves how far someone can go—and what he can accomplish once he gets there.

Series Glossary of Key Terms

All-star games: A game where the best players in the league form two teams and play each other.

Assist: A pass that leads to scoring points. The player who passes the ball before the other scores a basket gets the assist.

Center: A player, normally the tallest on the team, who tries to score close to the basket and defend against the other team's offense using his size.

Championship: A set of games between the two top teams in the NBA to see who is the best.

Court: The wooden or concrete surface where basketball is played. In the NBA, courts are 94 feet by 50 feet.

Defensive: Working to keep the other team from scoring points.

Draft (noun): The way NBA teams pick players from college or high school teams.

Foul: A move against another player that is against the rules, mostly involving a player touching another in a way that is not fair play.

Jump shot: A shot made from far from the basket (rather than under the basket) while the player is in the air.

Offensive: Working to score points against the other team.

Playoffs: Games at the end of the NBA season between the top teams in the league, ending in the finals, in which the two top teams play eachother.

Point guard: The player leading the team's offense, scoring points and setting up other players to score.

Power forward: A player who can both get in close to the basket and shoot from further away. On defense, power forwards defend against both close and far shots.

Rebound: Getting the ball back after a missed shot.

Rookie: A player in his first year in the NBA.

Scouts: People who search for new basketball players in high school or college who might one day play in the NBA.

Shooting guard: A player whose job is to take shots from far away from the basket. The shooting guard is usually the team's best long-range shooter.

Small forwards: Players whose main job is to score points close to the basket, working with the other players on the team's offense.

Steal: Take the ball from a player on the other team.

Tournament: A series of games between different teams in which the winning teams move on to play other winning teams and losing teams drop out of the competition.

Find Out More

ONLINE

Dwyane Wade's Official Website
dwyanewade.com

Dwyane Wade on ESPN.com
espn.go.com/nba/player/_/id/1987/dwyane-wade

Dwyane Wade on NBA.com
www.nba.com/playerfile/dwyane_wade

Dwyane Wade (THREE) on Twitter
twitter.com/DwyaneWade

IN BOOKS

Doeden, Matt. *Dwyane Wade: Basketball Superstar (Superstar Athletes)*. New York: Sports Illustrated Kids, 2014.

Glaser, Jason. *Dwyane Wade (Today's Sports Greats)*. New York: Gareth Stevens Publishing, 2011.

Keith, Ted. *Dwyane Wade (World's Greatest Athletes)*. North Mankato, Minn.: Child's World, 2008.

Sandler, Michael. *Dwyane Wade (Basketball Heroes Making a Difference)*. New York: Bearport Publishing, 2012.

Smallwood, John. *Dwyane Wade (NBA Reader)*. New York: Scholastic Inc., 2007.

Index

About the Author

Aurelia Jackson is a writer living and working in New York City. She has a passion for writing and a love of education, both of which she brings to all the work she does.

Picture Credits